by A.D. Walton

Published by Newcastle upon Tyne City
Libraries & Arts

Acknowledgements:
The photographs in this book are reproduced by kind permission of the following:

CityRepro (16)
Mr Forsyth/West Newcastle Local Studies (4, 11, 14)
Newcastle upon Tyne City Libraries & Arts (1, 6, 9, 12, 13, 20, 21)
Mr Quinn (18)
Mr Walton (front cover)
West Newcastle Local Studies (2, 3, 5, 7, 8, 10, 15, 17, 19)

Front Cover:
Knocking-off time on Scotswood Road as workmen leave Armstrong's Works on the left. Part of the wall of the Elswick Works Institute and School is on the right. The bridge led from Low Elswick Pit adjoining Glue House Lane off right and was part of a waggonway to a jetty on the river. The pit closed during World War Two and this view was in 1910.

Published by Newcastle upon Tyne City Libraries & Arts
©City of Newcastle upon Tyne, Newcastle Libraries & Arts, Leisure Services Department, 1992

ISBN 1 85795 010 0

Prior to being incorporated into Newcastle in 1835 Elswick was a Northumberland township which had been made a part of the Barony of Bolam after the Norman Conquest. A recorded spelling in 1292 was *Elstewyk*, during the time it was owned by Tynemouth Priory (1120 to the dissolution in 1539). The monks had a fishery at Elswick, received yearly dues from copyhold cultivators and benefitted from the letting of coal mines from as early as 1330. The export of Elswick coal to London via Tynemouth from seams near the surface helped to initiate the lucrative Tyneside coal trade.

Elswick lay between the west walls of Newcastle and the township of Benwell, and north from the river to the Nuns Moor. The hamlet of Westgate in the north east of Elswick became a separate township in 1662, mainly for poor law purposes. Elswick was owned by the Crown from 1539 to 1628, when it was sold by Charles I. Soon afterwards land was resold to the Jenisons of Newcastle and the Ords of the neighbouring township of Fenham. During the 1644 siege of Newcastle the Scots used Elswick pitmen to help to undermine the town walls and during the siege an island alongside Elswick, the mile long King's Meadows, was used by the Scots to patrol the Tyne. The island was dredged away by the Tyne Commissioners by 1887 and a block of flats near Brunel Terrace now bears the name. Neighbouring flats are called Haughton Court, after the name of the Northumberland home of the Cruddas family who had once lived in Elswick Dene House nearby.

The Priors had a mansion in the middle of Elswick and later owners lived on the site in Elswick Hall, rebuilt several times. The last hall was built by John Hodgson in 1810 and its grounds became Elswick Park in 1881. A fountain in the park today commemorates the names of a group of men who purchased land before 1881 to avoid it being built on and then transferred it to Newcastle Corporation. One was W.H. Stephenson of Elswick House, industrialist, politician and benefactor. Occupants of Elswick Hall included the builder Richard Grainger and the chemical industrialist Christian Allhusen. Between 1877 and 1930 the hall was known as the "Model House" when it contained work by the local sculptor, John Graham Lough. A noted Quaker family, the Richardsons of Elswick Leather Works, lived locally, including one home on Elswick Road, "The Gables", which is now Hopedene Hostel.

Westgate Road was built on the line of the Roman Wall and the part of Elswick to the north of the road was originally known as North or High Elswick. An estate built in the 1820s where the tall flats now stand took the name Arthur's Hill after the name of the son of estate owner Isaac Cookson. First streets in it were named after his other three sons and Arthur's Hill became the name of the area up to the General Hospital (originally Union Workhouse hospital). There is a tendency today to call it Fenham.

Elswick was completely transformed in the latter half of the 19th century. From 1839 the extension of the railway from Carlisle via Scotswood Railway Bridge through Low Elswick to Newcastle brought change, but the greatest change was inaugurated from 1847 by William Armstrong's purchase of 5½ acres in south west Elswick to manufacture hydraulic machinery and cranes. Population increased from 301 to 3,539 between 1801 and 1851, and by 1901 it had escalated to 59,165. After 1855 Elswick Works became known throughout the world because of Armstrong's invention of a revolutionary gun and projectile which combined breech loading with a rifled barrel, leading to export of armaments and warships. The ubiquitous Tyneside flats were quickly built on a gridiron pattern north from Scotswood Road to house the influx of workers. Early streets were named after engineers and politicians of the 1850s such as Brunel, Lord Herbert and Lord de Grey. Later streets were named after Richard Grainger's children, such as Isabella, Richard, Joseph and Stanley. By 1900 over 20,000 people worked for Armstrong and almost half the population of Newcastle lived in Westgate and Elswick.

Elswick's dependence on heavy industry and munitions had grave repercussions on a once thriving community when inter-war depression arrived. The large Victorian houses from Westmorland Road to Elswick Road could not be maintained as old families moved out, and multiple occupation began. The Second World War brought temporary prosperity but post-war modernisation proved impractical and employment at Vickers continued to drop. By 1964 the old Elswick had almost disappeared and families were housed in high rise flats or distant estates. The last ten years has seen the demolition of Elswick Works and the replacement of Scotswood Works with work for 750. The question we now ask is whether or not a new prosperity will return to the once proud Elswick through the designation of the site as part of an Enterprise zone and the subsequent construction of the Armstrong Industrial Centre and the Newcastle Business Park.

1. In 1992 the buildings in this 1906 view are similar in appearance. Marlborough Street was the name first given to the buildings on the left, later the beginning of Scotswood Road. Marlborough Crescent Bus Station was the sheep market here, left of tram. John Dobson designed the Cattle Market Exchange with clock tower, opened 1831.

2. The procession 'gannin' alang the Scotswood Road' on June 9th, 1962 is celebrating the centenary of the Tyneside anthem *The Blaydon Races*. Councillor Leslie Cuthbertson, Newcastle Centenary Committee chairman, doffs his topper as the horse bus passes the Cattle Market.

3. A charabanc trip is ready to leave George Street, off the beginning of Scotswood Road, in the 1920s and the pub is the George the First. There was much poverty in nearby streets during this period, caused by economic depression, as indicated by the onlookers on the left without shoes or stockings.

4. Scotswood Road photographer Jimmy Forsyth captured this scene in April, 1967, while Elswick East Terrace houses built in the 1830s were being demolished. A new aspect of once imposing Rye Hill appeared, as well as the St Mary the Virgin church, Cambridge Street School, and above it the new Charles Trevelyan building of the College of Arts and Technology (now Newcastle College).

5. This building was occupied by the Royal Grammar School between 1870 and 1907. Here it is occupied by Rutherford Girls' School, Maple Terrace, before moving to the West Road in 1958. Newcastle College is now on the site but a hostel for men still stands nearby in the old St Mary the Virgin Hospital buildings.

6. During the 1938 war scare sandbags were placed in front of the Throat, Nose and Ear Hospital on the corner of Rye Hill and Westmorland Road. The building is used by Newcastle College in 1992.

7. Todd Brothers was the largest store on Scotswood Road, at 176/196, and stood at the bottom of Maple Street. It was noted for its wide variety of goods and for its credit business employing 'ticket' or 'tally' men. This 1910 view looks west along Scotswood Road to the bottom of Gloucester Street.

8. Pine Street ran between Park Road and Maple Street and other nearby streets were named after trees, e.g. Laurel, Sycamore and Oak. In this 1905 view a charabanc waits in Pine Street to leave on an outing and the smartly dressed boys looking on may be in their Sunday best to attend Sunday School.

9. The street party is being held in Mill Street, below and parallel with Scotswood Road, to celebrate the Silver Jubilee of King George V in May, 1935. Some head bands are reminiscent of uniform worn by 'Nippies' when serving in restaurants. Dunn Street Methodist Mission stands at the end.

10. Richardson's Leather works (1863-1970) was situated below Scotswood Road and the railway. Employees lived adjoining the works in Water Street, Railway Street and Shumac Street. After work parents sat near their greenhouses in the shadow of factory buildings while children played.

11. The Grapes Hotel, 450, Scotswood Road, lay at the bottom of Hawes Street opposite Low Elswick post office (right). These were the first streets to be cleared for high rise flats and had been named after engineers and government ministers of the 1850s, e.g. Brunel, Lord de Grey (street at top), Lord Herbert, Clumber (Nottingham estate of the Duke of Newcastle).

12. Vickers, previously Armstrongs, Elswick Works stretched for over a mile alongside the Tyne from the boundary with Benwell to Water Street in the foreground, c1950. Streets and works have gone but St John's cemetery, top right, remains and St Stephen's spire, centre right, is still a landmark among high rise flats even though a new church building is detached from the tower.

13. The island King's Meadows, one mile long, lay off Elswick and was dredged away by 1887. Could this be the last remnant? In 1887 Sir W.G. Armstrong, Mitchell & Co. Ltd. was building the ill-fated HMS *Victoria*, one of the first ships on the Elswick stocks, with St Stephen's church behind.

14. A view of Cruddas Park School in a corner of the park with the pub The Dene to the left at the bottom of Georges Road — the slope of the latter can be seen right. Like Cambridge Street School the playground was on the roof. A police box and fountain are attached to the park wall, Scotswood Road.

15. Armstrong's men on a day off c1920. Some wear the regulation flat caps and mufflers and foremen can be distinguished by their bowlers and watch chains. They stand at the corner of Scotswood Road and Georges Road and higher up the latter stood Elswick Dene House, once home of the Cruddas family and now a men's home.

16. Elswick Hall, built in 1810, still lay in the park in October, 1975. It was once known as the 'Model House' when it housed the models of local sculptor John Lough. In 1981 it was replaced by swimming baths. Further left among trees is the roof of St Anne's Girls' School, previously Elswick House when the home of Sir William Stephenson.

17. Sir W.H. Stephenson (1836-1918) presented this building to the city in 1896 as its first branch library. It became West End Leisure and Learning in 1984. He also helped to found the Methodist Church right, pictured in this 1908 postcard. It ceased to be a church in 1970 when it was purchased by the Pakistan Muslim community.

18. It was unusual to see family picnic groups like this in Elswick Park in the 1950s so soon after Partition in India. The bandstand had not always stood here, next to Elswick Road, with Mill Lane in the background right. The address of the Co-op behind was 4, Bentinck Crescent and the building is now a hotel.

19. The Woodbine Laundry stood just east of St John's cemetery on Elswick Road and was preceded on the site by Woodbine Villa — now there is housing there. In 1913 the pony and trap was used to tour houses to collect items for cleaning and later delivery back.

20. Two Edwardian ladies are waiting on Elswick Road, near the end of Malvern Street, for a tram into town. On the road opposite them are signs of the passage of a horse and cart. On the left are John Knox Presbyterian Church, Beech Grove Road, Lloyd's Bank and the Stephenson Library. On the right is Elswick Road Wesleyan Methodist Church. Both churches have since been demolished.

21. The junction ahead is still known as the 'Big Lamp'. This 1910 postcard was taken from the beginning of Elswick Road and the view in 1992 is little changed. The corner of Westgate Hill cemetery is on the left, the tall building was Westgate Hall Methodist Mission and Stewardson's chemist shop then stood at the corner of Lancaster Street, right.